Drawing by Gaetano Piccini, 1727, of the excavation of the statue of Hercules, *Albertina, Vienna*

D1484938

Art and Archaeology

Shirley Glubok

Designed by Gerard Nook

HARPER & ROW, PUBLISHERS • NEW YORK

Hercules.
National Gallery of
Antiquities, Parma

Siskiyou County Schools Library
E.S.E.A. TITLE II, PHASE TWO, 1969

Discovery of the statue of Augustus of the Prima Porta, Rome,
The Metropolitan Museum of Art, Whittlesey Fund, 1955

THE AUTHOR GRATEFULLY ACKNOWLEDGES THE ASSISTANCE OF:

DONALD W. BRADEEN, Professor of Classics and Ancient History, University of Cincinnati

OTTO J. BRENDEL, Professor of Art History and Archaeology, Columbia University

PRUDENCE HARPER, Assistant Curator, Department of Near Eastern Art, The Metropolitan Museum of Art

ASCHWIN LIPPE, Associate Curator in Charge of Far Eastern Art, The Metropolitan Museum of Art

PAUL S. MARTIN, Chief Curator Emeritus of Anthropology, Chicago Natural History Museum

GEORGE E. MYLONAS, Professor of Art and Archaeology, and Distinguished Professor in the Humanities, Washington University

JOHN A. POPE, Director, Freer Gallery of Art

GEORGE I. QUIMBY, Curator of North American Archaeology and Ethnology, Chicago Natural History Museum

LINTON SATTERTHWAITE, Curator, American Section, The University Museum, University of Pennsylvania

MARGARET R. SCHERER, Former Research Associate, The Metropolitan Museum of Art

ERIC YOUNG, Assistant Curator, Department of Egyptian Art, The Metropolitan Museum of Art

Master PAUL SCHNELL

ART AND ARCHAEOLOGY—Copyright © 1966 by Shirley Glubok. Printed in the United States of America.
All rights reserved. No part of this book may be used or reproduced in any manner whatsoever without written permission
except in the case of brief quotations embodied in critical articles and reviews. For information address
Harper & Row, Publishers, Incorporated, 49 East 33rd Street, New York, N. Y. 10016.
Library of Congress Catalog Card Number: 65–11448

Augustus, *Vatican Museum, Alinari-Art Reference Bureau*

Everyone has, at one time or another, found some old object, picked it up, and wondered about it. How old is it? Who made it? How was it used? Who lost it?

All over the world, archaeologists find old objects and wonder about them. Archaeology is the discovery and study of ancient objects, to find out who made them, how they were used, and how they were lost. Things that are found are often all that is left to tell us about the forgotten past.

In some places whole cities have been found by archaeologists. Some had been destroyed by fire or by earthquakes, and some by war. Some cities had just been abandoned, to be covered by drifting sands or hidden by thick jungles.

Broken pottery, bits of stone and brick, or lost trinkets tell the archaeologist about the lives of ancient people. Once in a while, sometimes quite by accident, a great work of art that has been lost for hundreds of years may be discovered.

Chicago Natural History Museum

Siskiyou County Schools Library
E.S.E.A. TITLE II, PHASE TWO, 1969

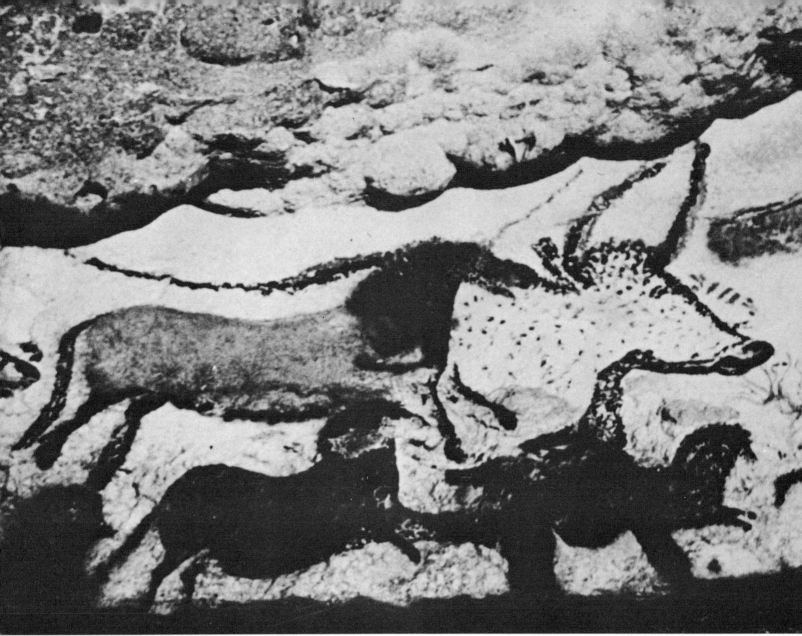

French Government Tourist Office

One day four boys and their dog were playing in the woods near Lascaux, in France. Suddenly their dog disappeared down a hole. One of the boys went into the hole to rescue his pet, and found himself in an underground cave.

The walls were covered with large, powerful paintings of animals. The boys had discovered a cave that had been used in the time of the Old Stone Age. Archaeologists think that the paintings may be more than fifteen thousand years old. The picture above shows a section of a wall in the Lascaux cave.

Prehistoric paintings in two other European caves were discovered by children—the caves of Altamira in Spain by a five-year-old girl, and Les Trois Frères in France by three brothers. Archaeologists, especially a French priest, the Abbé Henri Breuil, studied the paintings to learn about the lives and customs of Stone Age men, who made their tools and weapons of stone because they did not yet know about metals. The cavemen believed that their paintings served a magic purpose, to bring success when they went hunting for food.

A stray goat led to the discovery of the Dead Sea Scrolls. A young shepherd searching for his

goat along the rocky shores of the Dead Sea in Jordan came upon the entrance to a dark cave. He called a friend and they explored the cave together. They found rows of clay jars. Inside the jars were rolls of leather and papyrus, wrapped in linen. The rolls, or scrolls, were covered with ancient Hebrew writing.

The boys had discovered the earliest known Hebrew manuscripts of the Old Testament. The scrolls were brittle with age. Archaeologists worked with great care to keep them from crumbling into dust. In this photograph a scholar is studying fragments of the Dead Sea Scrolls through a magnifying glass.

American Friends of the Hebrew University

5

The Bible tells the story of the fall of Jericho, a town in Jordan north of the Dead Sea. Joshua and the Hebrew people had to capture Jericho before they could settle down in the Land of Canaan, known as the Promised Land. They marched around and around the walls of Jericho. They shouted and blew their trumpets until the walls came tumbling down.

Archaeologists have been digging at Jericho for about a hundred years. They have found part of a small house from the town Joshua captured about thirty-five hundred years ago. Deeper in the ground are remains of earlier settlements. The picture on the left shows a workman on a village wall that is eight thousand years old.

Kathleen Kenyon, an English archaeologist, dug even deeper and found a prehistoric settlement still a thousand years older. Jericho may be the oldest town in the world. It was a settled community in the New Stone Age, almost nine thousand years ago, more than fifty-five hundred years before Joshua blew his trumpets.

Not far from Jericho is the village of El Jib. James Pritchard dug, or excavated, there and was able to prove that this was the Biblical town of Gibeon, where Joshua won another battle.

Other stories from the Bible are coming to life under the careful excavations of Nelson Glueck, who discovered King Solomon's mines, and of Yigael Yadin, who dug at Hazor. Hazor is an ancient city in northern Israel, which the Bible says was destroyed by Joshua and rebuilt by Solomon.

Excavations have also revealed towns that existed in ancient Palestine in more recent times. This mosaic floor design dates from the sixth century A.D. It was found in the ruins of a synagogue at Nirim, Israel.

Courtesy of Israel Department of Antiquities

Copyright, Jericho Excavation Fund

The University Museum,
University of Pennsylvania

The ancient land of Mesopotamia lay in the fertile valley between the Tigris and Euphrates rivers in southwest Asia. It is often called the cradle of civilization. The earliest people we know who lived in Mesopotamia were the Sumerians, who inhabited the land five thousand years ago. Their civilization was totally forgotten for thousands of years until, in the late nineteenth century, it was discovered by archaeologists.

Then in the nineteen twenties Sir Leonard Woolley, an English archaeologist, excavated at Ur, the birthplace of Abraham, who is known in the Bible as the first Hebrew. Under tons of rubbish, broken bricks, and bits of pottery Woolley found two cemeteries, one on top of the other. In the lower burial ground he unearthed the tombs of sixteen kings and queens. Altogether there were more than two thousand graves of the royal families and their subjects.

The Royal Cemetery at Ur was the burying place of Sumerian kings. When a king died, his favorite attendants, servants, and musicians went to the grave with him. It seems that they walked into the tomb, lined themselves up in neat rows, and then drank a cup of poison so that they would be with their king and master forever. Animals dragging heavy chariots down a ramp into the grave were also buried with the king.

When Woolley and his workmen uncovered the tombs, they found beautiful headdresses, earrings, and necklaces on the women in the graves. One woman, a handmaiden to the queen, had a tightly coiled silver hair ribbon in her pocket. Perhaps she was late and did not have time to put it on before the final ceremony.

Among the treasures found in the Royal Tombs were the remains of a wooden harp decorated with a gold bull's head. The shell plaque at the left was on the sound box of the harp. The top panel shows a hero with two human-headed bulls, and below it a lion and a wolf are serving at a table. In the third panel a donkey is playing a harp with a bull's head decoration. The strange person in the bottom panel is part man, part scorpion. A scorpion man guarded the place of the sunrise in an ancient Sumerian fable.

These stone statues were found in another Sumerian town, now called Tell Asmar. The figures are worshipers. They were buried together under the floor of a temple, beside the altar. Sumerian statues were believed to possess a life of their own. The figures shown below have had their hands clasped in prayer for nearly five thousand years.

Courtesy of the Oriental Institute, University of Chicago

Courtesy of The Metropolitan Museum of Art

Long after the Sumerians, the warlike Assyrians built a mighty empire with its seat in northern Mesopotamia. The powerful Assyrian empire came to an end about twenty-five hundred years ago. Its cities with their great palaces were destroyed. The mud-brick walls collapsed and the roofs fell in. After a time only large mounds of earth showed where the great palaces had once stood.

For twenty-four centuries nothing was known about Assyria except for a few references in the Bible and some small mention by ancient historians. Finally, a little over a hundred years ago, a young Englishman, Sir Austen Henry Layard, began to dig into a mound at Nimrud.

As a boy, he had pored over the pages of the *Arabian Nights* and dreamed of travels and adventures in the Near East. When he was older he had an adventurous journey to that part of the world, wandering about, studying, and exploring. Almost as soon as he began to excavate in Nimrud, he unearthed the palace of Ashurnasirpal, a mighty king of Assyria. The walls of the palace were covered with large blocks of stone which were carved with pictures and stories of the king's mighty deeds and the power of his gods.

The powerful statue on the right was found guarding a doorway in the buried palace. It combines a winged bull with a human head. The statue represents the strength of a bull and an eagle, and the wisdom of man. The figure has a fifth leg. When seen from the side, four legs show and it seems to stride forward. Seen from the front, two legs show and the statue seems calm but alert, ready to guard the doorway from all evil and to protect the king within. The figure is carved from a single block of stone and weighs about eight tons.

In Layard's time photography was not yet developed, so Layard could not take photographs of his excavations, as archaeologists do today. However, he was skillful at drawing pictures and he sketched the scene on the left showing one of the great winged statues being moved during the excavations. The bull is being lowered by ropes onto a specially built platform, to be rolled across miles of desert, put on a ship, and taken to a museum for all the world to see. Layard drew himself in the picture. He is the man at the top of the mound directing the workmen. He used the sketch to illustrate a book that he wrote, *Nineveh and Its Remains.*

The Metropolitan Museum of Art, gift of John D. Rockefeller, Jr., 1932, photograph by Alfred H. Tamarin

11

Soon after the downfall of the Assyrians a new empire grew up in southwest Asia under the Persians. Persepolis, an entire city of magnificent palaces, was built by powerful Persian kings, in the land that is now Iran. Four kings built Persepolis over a period of about one hundred and seventy years. The palaces were erected on a huge stone terrace set at the foot of a mountain. On this terrace the kings built high, square rooms that were used as throne rooms, audience halls, and treasuries, as well as living quarters for the royal families.

Some of the stone pillars of the palaces were sixty feet high, the tallest columns ever built in the ancient world. They supported roofs made of cedar decorated with precious metals. One room had over a hundred of these lofty stone columns.

Great staircases led up to the terrace and some of the palaces. One was so wide that ten horsemen riding abreast could easily move up the sloping stairs. The staircases were decorated with rows of carved figures which glorified the "King of Kings," as the Persian rulers were called.

In the year 331 B.C. Alexander the Great led his army against Darius of Persia and defeated him. As part of his victory celebration, Alexander let his soldiers wreck and burn Persepolis. The soldiers carried off the treasures, and the palaces went up in flames.

Modern archaeologists led by Erich F. Schmidt of the University of Chicago have uncovered most of the remains of the palaces at Persepolis. Now it is again possible to see the towering columns that once supported the palace roofs. The view on the left shows the stone pillars, still standing against the background of the Mountain of Mercy. The great staircases are decorated with long rows of carvings showing Persian and foreign nobles, warriors, and servants bringing tribute to the Persian kings. The carving of the lion and the bull below is on the sweeping staircase leading to an audience hall.

Erich F. Schmidt,
Oriental Institute,
University of Chicago

The richest treasure ever uncovered by archaeologists was found in an Egyptian tomb that was buried for thirty-three centuries. The tomb belonged to Tutankhamun, a boy king of Egypt who died when he was about eighteen years old. It was discovered by an expedition led by two Englishmen, Howard Carter and the Earl of Carnarvon.

For five seasons the archaeologists had searched the Valley of the Tombs of the Kings on the west bank of the Nile River. They worked carefully month after month, season after season, but found almost nothing. Just as they were about to give up and were thinking of leaving the valley, they came upon the carefully hidden tomb cut into the side of a small, rocky hill. In the photograph on the opposite page the entrance to the tomb of Tutankhamun is to the left of the boxes and be-

hind the stone wall in the lower foreground.

As they cleared away the entrance, the archaeologists found sixteen steps leading down to a door. The door had been stamped with the royal seal of King Tutankhamun as well as other seal impressions from a slightly later time. Archaeologists believe that in ancient times robbers had broken into the tomb and later it had been resealed.

Archaeologists take hundreds of photographs showing every step of their excavations. The photograph below was taken just after the inner storage chamber in Tutankhamun's tomb was opened. The animal on the chest, covered with linen, is a magnificent statue of the jackal god of Egypt, Anubis. The numbers were put on the objects to keep track of them and the positions where they were found. The inner storage

Photographs by Harry Burton, The Metropolitan Museum of Art

Photograph by Harry Burton, The Metropolitan Museum of Art

chamber was found in disorder. Apparently, ancient tomb robbers had broken in, but it seems that they were caught before they could steal anything.

Tutankhamùn's tomb was filled with hundreds of treasures. Some were breathtakingly beautiful. This statue of the goddess Neith was one of the four guardian goddesses in the tomb. It is made of wood and covered with gold.

In another chamber Carter found Tutankhamun's sarcophagus, a stone chest that contained the mummy. The lid of the sarcophagus, weighing a ton and a quarter, was lifted, and three coffins were found one inside the other. The inner-

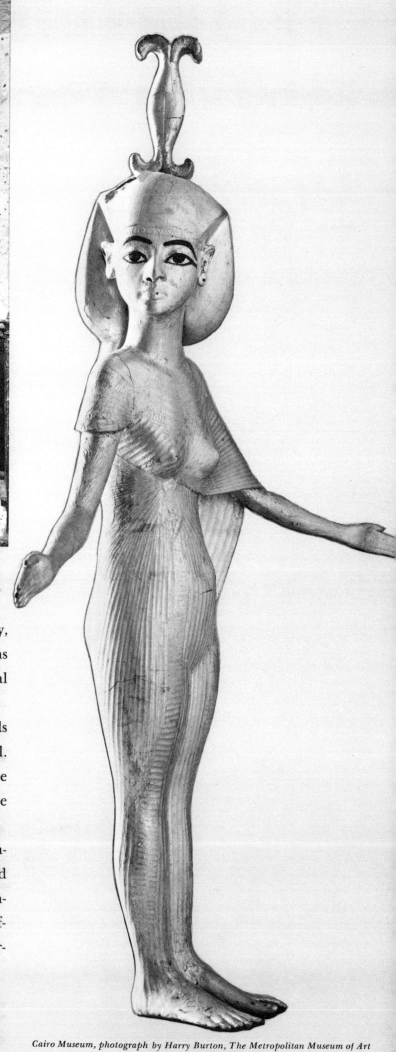

Cairo Museum, photograph by Harry Burton, The Metropolitan Museum of Art

most coffin is solid gold and weighs over nine hundred pounds.

On the right is the gold mummy mask that covered Tutankhamun's face. The mask is a likeness of the boy king wearing a false beard. The cobra and vulture on his royal headdress are symbols of the two kingdoms that he ruled over, Upper and Lower Egypt. Never before had archaeologists found a royal mummy undisturbed by grave robbers. Now for the first time they were able to see the full splendor of a royal Egyptian burial.

A great ceremony was held when Tutankhamun's tomb was opened. Leading Egyptologists and important government officials were invited. Many newspapers sent reporters, and people all over the world waited for the story.

The man in the photograph working on the coffin is Howard Carter.

*Cairo Museum, photograph by **Carol Guyer***

*Photograph by **Harry Burton**, The Metropolitan Museum of Art*

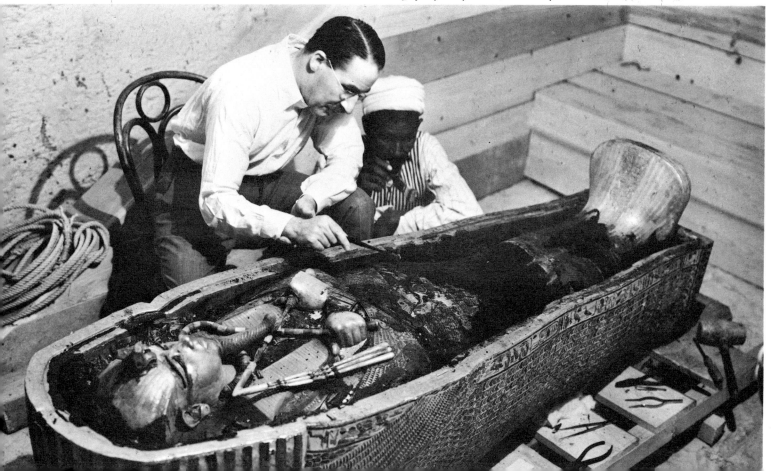

Another king of ancient Egypt, who ruled before Tutankhamun, was really a queen. Women were not supposed to rule. Nevertheless Queen Hatshepsut seized the throne and declared that she was king.

Hatshepsut was the daughter of King Thutmose I. When he died and was buried in the Valley of the Tombs of the Kings, Hatshepsut and her husband, Thutmose II, ruled as king and queen. Then when Thutmose II died, Hatshep-

The Metropolitan Museum of Art,
Rogers Fund, 1929,
photograph by Alfred H. Tamarin

Photograph by Egyptian Expedition, The Metropolitan Museum of Art

sut's stepson, Thutmose III, was named his successor. But since the new king was a mere child, Hatshepsut was entrusted to act as ruler until the boy became of age. However, Hatshepsut took over the throne, and she had herself crowned Pharaoh, King of Upper and Lower Egypt.

Soon work was begun on her enormous temple at Deir el Bahri. It was built at the foot of a gigantic cliff in the Egyptian desert. The sanctuary, or sacred part of the temple, was actually carved into the mountain wall at the side of the cliff.

A long avenue approached the temple and the three courts that led into the sanctuary. Hatshepsut ordered more than two hundred statues of herself to be made, to line the avenue, decorate the columns, and show her in all the poses of a king. Some showed her head on the body of a lion, as a sphinx. Most showed her wearing the false beard of a king. The statue on the left is one of the few that shows Hatshepsut as a woman.

Hatshepsut's stepson was bitter because she had seized the throne. When she died he decreed that her name be erased from the temple. But he did not destroy the great temple, because it was dedicated to the god Amun, king of all gods in Egypt. He ordered all the statues in her temple to be smashed to bits and thrown into a quarry. For thirty-four hundred years the desert sand gradually drifted over the temple.

In the late nineteenth century a British expedition began to excavate. They thought a nearby quarry was a good place to dump the sand and dirt that they cleared away from the temple.

A few years later the Metropolitan Museum of Art sent a party under the direction of Herbert E. Winlock to excavate in Deir el Bahri. The expedition cleared out the dirt that had been dumped into the quarry and found pieces of Hatshepsut's statues. Many pieces were also found in holes on either side of the temple avenue. Some of the workmen in Thutmose III's day had been too lazy to carry them to the quarry, so they had dumped them along the way.

The pieces were like a hundred jigsaw puzzles all mixed together. Some were as little as a fingertip. Others were so large and heavy that they could only be moved by derricks, as shown in the picture below.

Although they were broken up, many of the statues were otherwise in good condition. The paint was still fresh on some of them because the statues had been buried when they were still

Photograph by Egyptian Expedition, The Metropolitan Museum of Art

The Metropolitan Museum of Art, Rogers Fund, 1930, photograph by Alfred H. Tamarin

new. Each piece of statue was carefully recorded and numbered and sent to Cairo or to the Metropolitan Museum in New York.

Figures like this one stood at the sides of one of the courts in the temple. The Pharaoh Hatshepsut is kneeling before her god and holding a small round offering jar, for wine, in each hand. Like the other statues, this one was smashed to pieces and scattered far and wide. It was carefully put back together in the Metropolitan Museum's workshop, and missing parts were filled in.

buried ruins, layer upon layer, of many cities built one on top of the other. Almost thirty feet below the surface he found the remains of buildings and metal objects that showed traces of having been destroyed by a fire.

On the very last day of his excavations Schliemann dug up a treasure trove of golden jewelry and ornaments. He claimed that it was the treasure of Priam, king of Homer's Troy. Sophie Schliemann is shown here wearing the golden jewels and necklaces which her husband thought had belonged to Helen, the beautiful queen over whom the Trojan War was fought. This photograph of Schliemann was taken in 1861, before he went to Troy.

Over a hundred years ago in a little town in Germany a young boy read and reread *The Iliad* and *The Odyssey*, Homer's heroic poems about ancient Troy and the long war between the Greeks and the Trojans. For centuries people had believed that these stories were imaginary.

The young German lad, named Heinrich Schliemann, vowed that one day he would find the buried ruins of Ilium, as ancient Troy was called, and would prove it was real.

Many years later Schliemann began digging in a mound called Hissarlik, on the Turkish coast of the Aegean Sea. Soon he came upon

Photographs courtesy of Dr. Ernst Meyer, Berlin

German Archaeological Institute, Athens

Schliemann is sometimes called the Father of Archaeology. He was the first man to dig scientifically in order to learn about the early history of mankind. Earlier excavators were usually searching for buried gold or art treasures.

In recent years archaeologists from the University of Cincinnati, led by Carl W. Blegen, have renewed excavations at the site of ancient Troy. The photograph above shows the towers and walls of nine layers of buried cities. The Troy of Priam's time is now believed to be the seventh layer from the bottom, a thousand years later than the layer that Schliemann thought was Priam's Troy. It is called Troy VIIa.

*National Museum, Athens,
photograph by Alison Frantz*

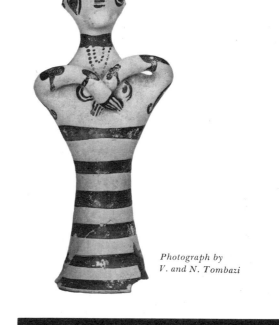

*Photograph by
V. and N. Tombazi*

Schliemann is the seated man wearing a hat in the lower left of the photograph on the opposite page. The photograph was taken at the famous Lion Gate in Mycenae on the mainland of Greece. Schliemann had come to search for King Agamemnon, leader of the Greeks in the Trojan War. He found a large circular area in which he discovered five rectangular graves of Mycenaean kings, filled with treasures. A sixth grave was found after he left.

The bronze dagger above, decorated with gold inlaid figures of animals and warriors, is from Schliemann's excavations at Mycenae.

Schliemann also found five beautiful gold masks and thought that one of these was the funeral mask of Agamemnon. But it is now known to be from an earlier time. Schliemann was the first to uncover the Mycenaean civilization, one of the most brilliant civilizations that developed on the Greek mainland. It began nearly four thousand years ago and lasted for nearly a thousand years.

Excavations still continue at Mycenae under the direction of George E. Mylonas. The little terra cotta figure of an ancient Mycenaean goddess is one of his recent finds.

National Museum, Athens, photograph by V. and N. Tombazi

There is a Greek legend about Theseus, a young prince of Athens. He was sent to Crete to be devoured by the Minotaur, a monster, half man, half bull. King Minos kept the Minotaur hidden in an underground labyrinth, a maze of twisting paths. Theseus went into the labyrinth and killed the Minotaur. He found his way out of the maze by following a trail of thread which had been given to him by King Minos's daughter Ariadne.

At Knossos on the island of Crete, Sir Arthur Evans found the ruins of a great palace. Representations of bulls were painted everywhere. Sir Arthur named the civilization Minoan, after the legendary Cretan King Minos.

Walls of the Minoan palaces were decorated

Heraklion Museum, photograph by Alison Frantz

with gay, lively figures. The wall painting above shows slim young people doing somersaults over the back of a charging bull. On the right is a portrait of Sir Arthur Evans.

The Minoan civilization existed at the same time as the mainland civilization of Mycenae. The Minoans built their palaces with tapered columns that were wider at the top than at the bottom.

Sir Arthur Evans, painting by Sir William Richmond, *Ashmolean Museum*

27

pollo was the Greek god of light, and also the god of music, medicine, and archery. Over twenty-two hundred years ago in ancient Athens a small ivory figure of the god Apollo was dropped into a well. It was smashed into more than two hundred little pieces. As time went on the well was filled with earth. Twenty-two centuries later a team of American archaeologists, headed by T. Leslie Shear, were carefully digging in the old well, when slivers of ivory

began to appear in the muddy earth.

The tiny fragments were brittle with age. They had to be kept moist and treated with chemicals to preserve them.

The large photograph shows the fragments carefully laid out. It took a long time and a great deal of patience for the archaeologists to fit the pieces together. Some pieces were missing. They were replaced by bleached beeswax. Now the ivory Apollo is complete again.

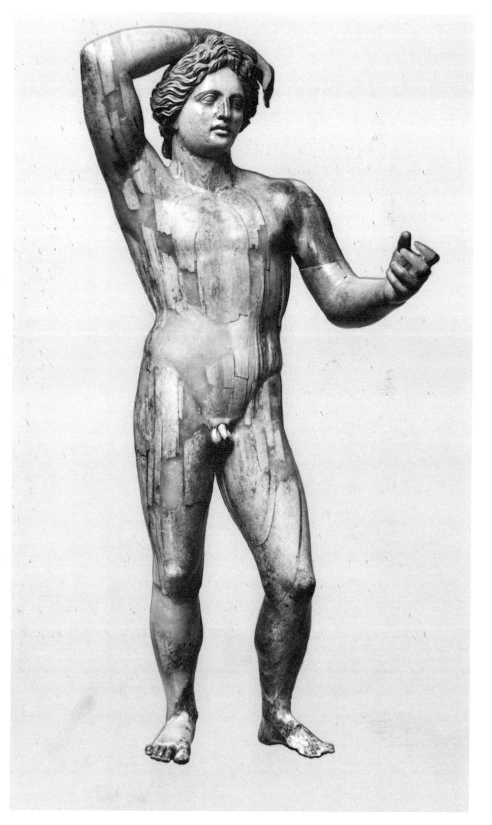

Agora Excavations

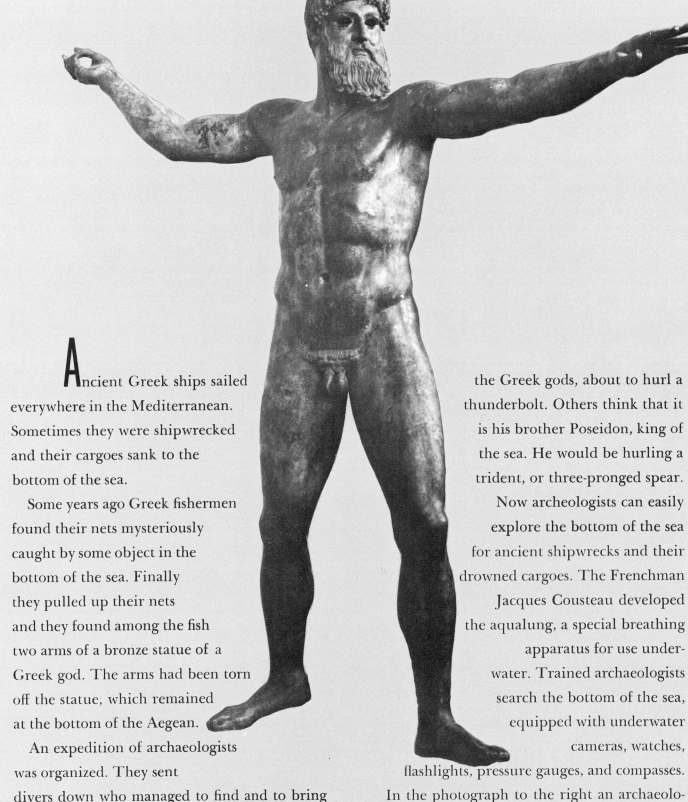

Ancient Greek ships sailed everywhere in the Mediterranean. Sometimes they were shipwrecked and their cargoes sank to the bottom of the sea.

Some years ago Greek fishermen found their nets mysteriously caught by some object in the bottom of the sea. Finally they pulled up their nets and they found among the fish two arms of a bronze statue of a Greek god. The arms had been torn off the statue, which remained at the bottom of the Aegean.

An expedition of archaeologists was organized. They sent divers down who managed to find and to bring up the rest of the statue, shown here. It is one of the great masterpieces of ancient Greek art. Some people think that it is a statue of Zeus, king of all the Greek gods, about to hurl a thunderbolt. Others think that it is his brother Poseidon, king of the sea. He would be hurling a trident, or three-pronged spear.

Now archeologists can easily explore the bottom of the sea for ancient shipwrecks and their drowned cargoes. The Frenchman Jacques Cousteau developed the aqualung, a special breathing apparatus for use underwater. Trained archaeologists search the bottom of the sea, equipped with underwater cameras, watches, flashlights, pressure gauges, and compasses.

In the photograph to the right an archaeologist, wearing an aqualung, is kneeling on the bottom of the sea. He is writing on plastic paper to keep a record of his work.

National Museum, Athens,
photograph by V. and N. Tombazi

The University Museum,
University of Pennsylvania,
courtesy of Peter Throckmorton

County Schools Library
PHASE TWO

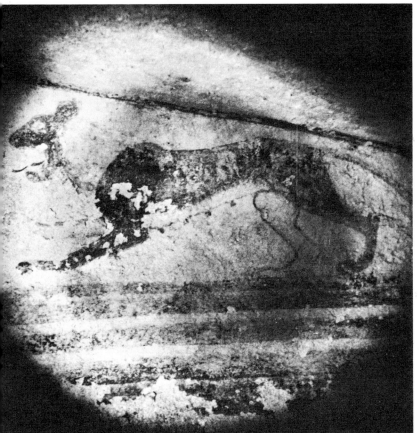

Photographs courtesy of Lerici Foundation

Many new scientific inventions help the archaeologist. The photograph at left shows an archaeologist looking into an underground tomb through a periscope. The periscope can be equipped with a camera to take pictures of an unopened tomb. The archaeologist can find out what is in the tomb before he starts to dig. The Etruscan wall painting below was photographed in an unopened tomb through a periscope.

The Etruscans are still one of the great puzzles of archaeology. They ruled a large part of Italy before the Romans rose to power. Nevertheless, no one is sure who the Etruscans were or where they came from.

The Etruscans built their tombs to look exactly like the insides of their homes. The houses of the living were built of wood or light materials. They have vanished. The houses of the dead are all that remain to give some idea of the people and their lives.

At the right is a photograph of the Tomb of the Reliefs. Household utensils are carved into the soft stone of the wall.

The terra cotta statue of an Etruscan man and his wife are on the lid of a sarcophagus found in an Etruscan tomb.

Villa Giulia, Rome, Alinari-Art Reference Bureau

Brogi-Art Reference Bureau

National Museum, Naples, Alinari-Art Reference Bureau

National Museum, Naples, Alinari-Art Reference Bureau

Pompeii was a gay and colorful city of ancient Rome, on the shores of the Mediterranean Sea. Its homes were filled with beautiful statues and decorated with fine wall paintings. One sunny summer day in A.D. 79 life was going on as usual, when Mt. Vesuvius, a live volcano near Pompeii, suddenly exploded. A huge cloud of hot vapor, fiery ashes, and molten rock poured down, darkening the sky and burying the city. Within three days all life was stopped. Pompeii was sealed underground and not seen again for seventeen hundred years.

Excavations were begun in Pompeii more than two hundred years ago. Archaeologists have reconstructed the town. At the right is a statue of Apollo as the god of archery, standing in front of the columns which surround his temple. Mt. Vesuvius looms in the background

Fortunately the volcanic ash that buried the city preserved the colors of the wall paintings. The painting above shows Cupid driving his chariot pulled by a pair of dolphins. The paint still looks fresh.

This mosaic picture of a chained dog was found in a doorway in Pompeii. The words "Cave Canem" mean "Beware of the dog."

Fototeca Unione, Rome

Ancient statues have often been dug up under the buildings and streets of modern Rome. Nearly a hundred years ago workmen digging out the foundations of a building came upon a magnificent bronze head. Archaeologists were immediately called in to supervise the digging. Slowly a large bronze statue was unearthed. It was seated on the capital, or top of a marble column. The photograph at the right was taken just as the statue seemed to be awakening from its long sleep.

The statue is a lifelike portrait of a boxer at rest. He has just finished a match and is sitting overcome with fatigue. The scars and cuts on his face and body show the results of many brutal boxing matches. It was probably made by a Greek artist some time after Greece had been conquered by Rome.

The archaeologists studied the sifted earth in which the statue had been buried. They came to the conclusion that the statue had been deliberately hidden underground to preserve it from harm. Most bronze statues of ancient Greece and Rome have not been preserved, because they were melted down for the precious metal.

Terme Museum, Rome,
Alinari-Art Reference Bureau   Photographed in 1885

Norwegian Information Service

The Vikings were a fierce and adventurous people of northern Europe, famous for their bold seamanship. In their long, sleek ships they sailed far and wide over the sea, making daring raids on neighboring lands.

In Oseberg, Norway, a seventy-one foot Viking ship was found buried in a bed of clay. The wetness of the ground preserved the ship and helped to keep the oak timbers from rotting. Archaeologists treated the timbers to harden them, and rebuilt the ship. The buried ship was the tomb of a Viking queen.

The Viking Ships Museum of the University of Oslo

*The Viking Ships Museum
of the University of Oslo*

Centuries ago tomb robbers had plundered some of the buried treasures. The finely carved wooden cart shown above was found untouched in the bow of the ship.

The photograph below shows the strange impressions left in the earth by an eighty-foot ship. It had been pulled ashore and buried under a mound of sand at Sutton Hoo, England. When it was found, the wood had rotted away. Nothing was left of the ship but the iron nails that had held the planking together. Yet archaeologists were able to tell how big the ship was and how it had been constructed.

A king's treasure of gold, silver, and jewels was found in the Sutton Hoo mound. There were also coins which showed that the ship had been buried soon after A.D. 650.

Courtesy of the British Museum

French School of Far Eastern Studies, Hanoi

Deep in the jungles of Cambodia, in southeast Asia, stands the huge temple city of Angkor. For centuries it was the capital city of the kingdom of the Khmers. About five hundred years ago, exhausted by wars and endless temple-building, the Khmers were conquered. Their great civilization began to disappear. Angkor was abandoned. The tropical jungle quickly moved in and took over. The magnificent buildings were overgrown. Tigers, panthers, and monkeys roamed through the corridors of the buildings.

Angkor was forgotten, although rumors of a lost city were sometimes heard. Travelers visiting Cambodia brought home tales that made people curious. Over a hundred years ago a Frenchman, Henri Mouhot, heard about the forgotten temples. He hacked his way through the dense jungle undergrowth and discovered Angkor. When he came upon it he could hardly believe his eyes.

Huge temples rising up like pyramids were covered over by thick trees and vines. Every bit of space on the walls was filled with rich carvings, and statues of gods and demons were everywhere.

Angkor Wat is the biggest and most magnificent of the temples, and it is the only one that was not completely overgrown by the forest. It was built by one of the powerful kings of Khmer, who expanded the kingdom by conquering his neighbors. The temple of Angkor Wat was for the worship of the Hindu god Vishnu and also served as a tomb for the king.

The temple is surrounded by a square moat, or deep ditch, each side of which is a mile long. A causeway, or raised road, leads across the moat up to the entrance of the temple. The moat is part of the waterway system that irrigated the rice paddies.

Every stone of the temples at Angkor is decorated with great care. The relief carving of two dancing girls is from the Bayon, the temple mountain in the center of the city of Angkor. The Bayon was used for the worship of the Buddha called Lokesvara. The walls of the Bayon are like a carved picture book, with miles of reliefs showing the glory of the Khmer kings, the strength of the armies, and the life of the people.

Now the jungle has been cleared away and parts of the ruins of Angkor have been rebuilt by French archaeologists. But some of the walls are still clutched by roots and branches.

Photographs by Carol Guyer

41

At Tikal, Guatemala, archaeologists from the University of Pennsylvania cleared away the dense jungle from the ruins of Maya temples built on top of pyramids. The one opposite is known as the Temple of the Giant Jaguar.

The beautiful jade head at the left was found in a tomb near the temple. It is just three and a half inches tall.

Maya pottery decorations tell us much about the lives and customs of the people. The vase below shows a seated priest making an offering to the gods. The vase is decorated with Maya glyphs, a form of picture writing which is not yet completely understood.

The Maya were another people whose civilization disappeared. Their buildings were also overgrown by the jungle. For hundreds of years great temples of the Maya were hidden by the tropical rain forests of Middle America. The Maya were a remarkable Indian people who lived in southern Mexico, Guatemala, and Honduras. Their great, or Classic, period runs from about 300 until about 900 A.D. The Maya understood the movements of the stars and planets, and they developed an excellent calendar system.

Photographs by The University Museum of the University of Pennsylvania

The Cleveland Museum of Art, The Norweb Collection

Machu Picchu, an Inca city high up on a peak in the Andes Mountains of Peru, was also abandoned. The Incas were the last of the great Indian civilizations of South America. In 1533 they were conquered by the Spanish.

Nearly four hundred years later an American explorer, Hiram Bingham, discovered the city, lost in the mountain mists, as seen below. Its walls and terraces are made of blocks of stone

Photograph by Martin Chambi

that are perfectly shaped. They are fitted together without mortar.

Earlier South American Indian peoples made beautiful fabrics. The mummy cloth at the left is painted with a design of a cat demon. It has been preserved for nearly two thousand years by the dry desert air of Peru.

The gold object at the right is also from ancient Peru. It is called a whistling jar because it whistles when water is poured out of it.

Dumbarton Oaks

The Dickerson Panorama,
*St. Louis City Art Museum, photograph
courtesy of The University Museum*

Many parts of North America are dotted with great mounds of earth built by early Indian tribes. Some of these mounds are curiously shaped. The Great Serpent Mound in Ohio is like a winding snake, over a thousand feet long. The Monk's Mound, in the Cahokia Group near St. Louis, is about one hundred feet high. The round mounds were for burial. The square mounds were bases for wooden temples which have rotted away. It took thousands of men to make these mounds.

The little figure on the left was found in the Adena Mound in Ohio. It is a stone pipe for smoking tobacco. The painting above shows excavations in an Indian mound in Louisiana.

Ohio Historical Society, Columbus, Ohio

Chicago Natural History Museum

The Pueblo Indians in the Southwest built stone houses of many stories and many rooms. In Arizona, Paul Martin from the Chicago Natural History Museum found an underground room called a *kiva*, which was used for religious ceremonies. Set into the floor of the room was a stone slab, covering a secret vault. When the archaeologists removed the slab, they found a clay pot with eleven beads in it and a little stone figure face down on the ground.

The archaeologists think that the figure was an Indian god, put in the vault for safekeeping. The little figure has only one arm. What happened to the other arm? Was it deliberately broken off?

Siskiyou County Schools Library
E.S.E.A. TITLE II, PHASE TWO, 1969

Chicago Natural History Museum

Archaeologists not only look for lost objects, they look for answers to all of the questions about the things they find. Archaeologists studied the stone Pueblo god and made a copy, with the lost arm replaced, to show how the god looked long ago. They also painted the copy with the green, yellow, red, and black stripes of the original.

Finding objects is just one part of the archaeologist's work. Studying the objects, comparing them, and restoring them to their original state are also parts of his work. In hundreds of ways archaeologists dig up things of the past to learn more and more about people of ancient times. It is our good fortune that archaeologists also discover great and beautiful works of art.

SISKIYOU CO. SUPT. SCHOOLS
LIBRARY
609 S. GOLD ST.
YREKA, CA 96097

#6079